D1030467

CONTENTS

Created by Romney Nelson

A Place to Share My Life Memories

THIS IS THE BEGINNING OF MY LIFE...

MY INTRODUCTION

Before I start....Just a brief introduction of me!

_____

_____

_____

_____

_____

_____

_____

_____

_____

Name:

Signature

Date

THE BEGINNING......

Full Name at Birth

_____

Date of Birth   / /

Time of Birth   :

Day of the week you were born?

Height at birth? (if known)

Weight at birth? (If known)

Your Place of Birth (include the City/Town, Country)

_____

Did you have any siblings when you were born? If so, what were their names and their ages?

_____

_____

ADD ANY ADDITIONAL NOTES OR INFORMATION HERE...

THE
BEGINNING......

Share with us some information about your parents?

_____

_____

_____

_____

_____

Were you in good health as a baby?

_____

_____

_____

Did you have any unique characteristics or funny things you did as a baby?

_____

_____

_____

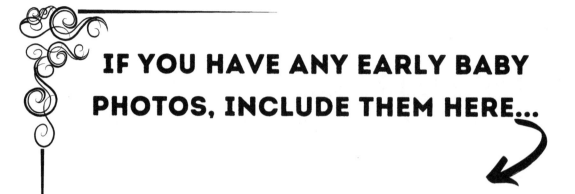

IF YOU HAVE ANY EARLY BABY PHOTOS, INCLUDE THEM HERE...

THE BEGINNING.....

Were you an active or quiet baby?

_____

Were you ever told what your first words were?

_____

_____

Do you have any other baby memories to share?

_____

_____

_____

_____

_____

_____

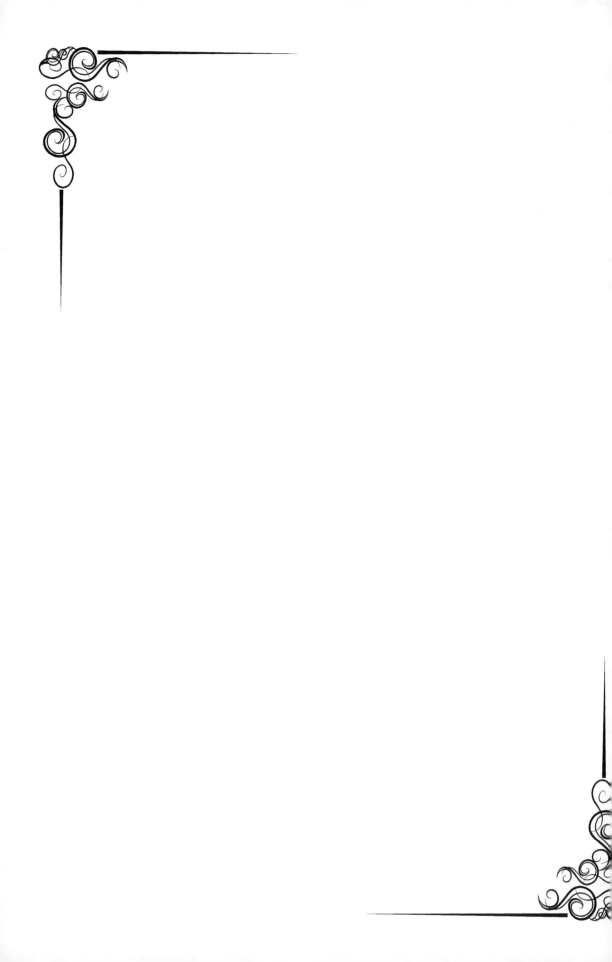

FAMILY HISTORY

This was our Family Tree!

FAMILY HISTORY

My grandparents names were:

Grandmother:

Grandfather:

They were born in: (country)
Grandmother:

Grandfather:

This is something that not many people may know abou
our family history......

Additional Family History information:

Our FAMILY TREE

GrandFather

GrandFather

Grandmother

Grandmother

Mother

Father

Me

ADD ANY ADDITIONAL NOTES OR INFORMATION HERE...

CHILDHOOD YEARS

CHILDHOOD YEARS....

What was your favorite toy growing up?

_____

_____

Did you have a pet or any pets growing up?

_____

_____

What was your favorite T.V show to watch as a child?

_____

_____

Was there a moment you remember getting into b
trouble as a child? Was there a punishment?

_____

_____

_____

_____

_____

_____

ADD ANY ADDITIONAL NOTES OR INFORMATION HERE...

CHILDHOOD YEARS....

What are your fondest memories growing up between the ages of 5 - 12 years?

_____

_____

_____

_____

_____

_____

_____

_____

_____

_____

IF YOU HAVE ANY EARLY CHILDHOOD PHOTOS, PLACE THEM HERE...

CHILDHOOD YEARS....

Where did you grow up as a child?
(house, location, town etc)

_____

_____

_____

_____

Who was your best friend or your best friends as a child?

_____

_____

What was your favorite day of the week and why?

_____

_____

_____

_____

CHILDHOOD YEARS....

What was your favorite meal as a child?

_____

What elementary/primary school did you attend and where was it located?

_____

_____

Describe your most memorable moment or story from elementary/primary school.

_____

_____

_____

_____

_____

_____

_____

_____

_____

_____

DO YOU HAVE ANY SCHOOL PHOTOS OR OTHER DETAILS TO SHARE?

TEENAGE YEARS

TEENAGE YEARS....

Describe your dress sense and clothing as a teenager. Is there anything that stands out for you?

_____

_____

_____

When and where did you learn to drive a vehicle?

_____

_____

What was your first vehicle and how much did you purchase it for? Tell us your special 'first car' story!

_____

_____

_____

_____

_____

_____

_____

INCLUE ANY 'FIRST VEHICLE' PHOTOS OR OTHER INFORMATION HERE..

TEENAGE YEARS....

What High School did you attend and where was it located?

_____
_____
_____

Who was you favorite teacher or coach and why?

_____
_____
_____

What was your favorite subject at school?

_____
_____
_____

Did you date anyone at High School?

_____
_____
_____
_____

SHARE ANY HIGH SCHOOL PHOTOS OR FURTHER DETAILS HERE

TEENAGE YEARS....

What hobbies did you have as a teenager?

_____

_____

What is your most memorable moment as a teenager?

_____

_____

_____

_____

_____

If you knew what you know today, what would you have done differently as a teenager?

_____

_____

_____

_____

_____

SHARE ANY HIGH SCHOOL PHOTOS OR OTHER DETAILS HERE

TEENAGE YEARS....

Did you have a close friendship group? Have you maintained contact with any of them?

_____

_____

_____

_____

_____

Did you have any nicknames at High School?

_____

_____

What 5 words come to mind to describe your teenage years?

1. _____

2. _____

3. _____

4. _____

5. _____

WHEN I WAS..

WHEN I WAS....

When I was a child, my mode of transport to school was...

_____

_____

When I was in my teens, the biggest news story that recall was .....

_____

_____

_____

When I was growing up, my 3 favorite movies were:

1. _____

2. _____

3. _____

WHEN I WAS....

When I was a child, the first movie I went to the theatre to see was..

_____

When I graduated from elementary/primary school, the year was.. _____

When I was a child, I wanted to be a......

_____

When I was 18 years old, my favorite music and band was..

_____

When I was in my teens, the most popular thing to do on a Saturday night was.......

_____

_____

When I was young, I loved to travel to.......

_____

_____

_____

SHARE ANY FURTHER TRAVEL MEMORIES HERE..

PARENTHOOD

PARENTHOOD....

How old were you when you first became a parent?

_____

Explain how you felt emotionally when you bacame parent for the first time?

_____

_____

_____

_____

_____

Where were you located (city/town/country) when yo had your first child?

_____

_____

_____

_____

SHARE SOME PARENTING PHOTOS HERE..

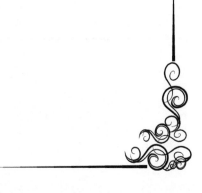

PARENTHOOD....

What has been the biggest challenge for you as a parent?

_____

_____

_____

_____

What are 3 key responsibilities you believe are important
as a parent?

1 _____

_____

2 _____

_____

3 _____

_____

 # PARENTHOOD....

EXPAND ON ANY FURTHER PARENTING
MEMORIES YOU MAY LIKE TO SHARE

_____

_____

_____

_____

_____

_____

_____

_____

_____

MORE ABOUT ME!

MORE ABOUT ME....

Not many people know this about me, so let me share with you:

_____

_____

_____

_____

_____

_____

_____

The activity or hobby that I enjoy most to do now is.....

_____

_____

I have the unique ability to be able to....

_____

_____

_____

MORE ABOUT ME....

I was able to go back to a special time in history, it
ould be...

_____

_____

_____

I could pass on one word of advice to others, it would
e..

_____

_____

_____

here are special moments in life that you wish you could
ause to enjoy for longer. Mine would be......

_____

_____

_____

_____

MORE ABOUT ME....

I wish I had the opportunity to...

_____

_____

_____

The quote that resonates most with me is..

_____

_____

_____

_____

My favorite book of all time is:

_____

If there is one thing I would like to be remembered for
would be:

_____

_____

_____

MORE ABOUT ME....

When I look back on my life so far, my 3 proudest moments are:

_____

_____

_____

If there were 3 famous people that I could invite for dinner they would be:

_____

_____

_____

MORE ABOUT ME....

From my teen years, these are the jobs that I've had:

_____

_____

_____

_____

_____

_____

_____

_____

_____

MORE ABOUT ME....

ne of the jobs that stands out as my most enjoyable has
een..

_____

_____

he most interesting place I have ever traveled to has
een.... (include the year/date this occurred)

_____

_____

_____

I was given a free return flight to anywhere in the
orld, I would visit...(include your 'Why')

_____

_____

_____

FINAL NOTES

FINAL NOTES....

There have been many questions that I have answered this book, but I would also like to share this with you...

Your time to write anything else you wis to share...

_____
_____
_____
_____
_____
_____
_____
_____
_____
_____
_____
_____
_____
_____
_____
_____
_____
_____
_____

INAL NOTES....

FINAL NOTES....

USE THE FOLLOWING PAGES FOR CERTIFICATES, AWARDS. PHOTO'S ETC..

USE THE FOLLOWING PAGES FOR CERTIFICATES, AWARDS. PHOTO'S ETC..

USE THE FOLLOWING PAGES FOR CERTIFICATES, AWARDS. PHOTO'S ETC..

THANK YOU FOR SHARING YOUR LIFE STORY

This book was created by

Romney Nelson

OTHER BOOKS

BY

Romney Nelson and The Life Graduate Publishing Group

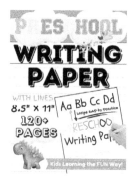

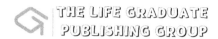

THE LIFE GRADUATE
PUBLISHING GROUP